DISCOVER AMERICA

IOWA

Jay D. Winans

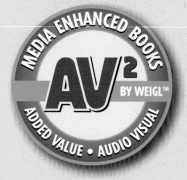

AV² provides enriched content that supplements and complements this book. Weigl's AV² books strive to create inspired learning and engage young minds in a total learning experience.

Your AV² Media Enhanced books come alive with...

Audio
Listen to sections of the book read aloud.

Key Words
Study vocabulary, and complete a matching word activity.

Video
Watch informative video clips.

Quizzes
Test your knowledge.

Embedded Weblinks
Gain additional information for research.

Slide Show
View images and captions, and prepare a presentation.

Go to **www.av2books.com,** and enter this book's unique code.

BOOK CODE

G 5 5 2 8 5 2

AV² by Weigl brings you media enhanced books that support active learning.

Try This!
Complete activities and hands-on experiments.

... and much, much more!

Published by AV² by Weigl
350 5th Avenue, 59th Floor
New York, NY 10118
Website: www.av2books.com

Library of Congress Cataloging-in-Publication Data
Names: Winans, Jay D., author.
Title: Iowa : the Hawkeye State / Jay D. Winans.
Description: New York, NY : AV2 by Weigl, [2016] | Series: Discover America | Includes index.
Identifiers: LCCN 2015048012 (print) | LCCN 2015048319 (ebook) | ISBN 9781489648600 (hard cover : alk. paper) | ISBN 9781489648617 (soft cover : alk. paper) | ISBN 9781489648624 (Multi-User eBook)
Subjects: LCSH: Iowa--Juvenile literature.
Classification: LCC F621.3 .W565 2016 (print) | LCC F621.3 (ebook) | DDC 977.7--dc23
LC record available at http://lccn.loc.gov/2015048012

Printed in the United States of America, in Brainerd, Minnesota
1 2 3 4 5 6 7 8 9 20 19 18 17 16

042016
040816

Project Coordinator Heather Kissock
Art Director Terry Paulhus

IOWA

Contents

OFFICIAL FLOWER
Wild Rose

STATE ROCK
Geode

STATE TREE
Oak

IOWA

STATE FLAG
Iowa

STATE BIRD
Eastern Goldfinch

Nickname
The Hawkeye State

Motto
Our Liberties We Prize, and
Our Rights We Will Maintain

Song
"The Song of Iowa," words by
S. H. M. Byers, sung to the tune
of "Der Tannenbaum"

Population
(2014 Census) 3,107,126,
ranked 30th state

OFFICIAL SEAL
Iowa

Capital
Des Moines

Entered the Union
December 28, 1846, as the 29th state

Discover Iowa

Iowa is located in the north-central area of the United States known as the Midwest. Roughly rectangular in shape, the state has rolling prairie farmland that stretches from the Mississippi River on the east to the Missouri River on the west. Vast cornfields and massive hog farms have supplied the country with food for decades. Iowa is often described as "one giant farm," with businesses that handle all aspects of the agricultural process, from harvesting crops to packaging foods. Its rich soils nourish some of the most abundant crops in the world.

More than just farmland, Iowa has many state parks, museums, and tourist attractions. The Grout Museum District in Waterloo, Iowa, is a unique area that works to honor the history of the area. The state offers outdoor enthusiasts more than 1,800 miles of biking trails throughout the state parks. Madison County is home to six famous covered bridges. Visitors to the area can join tours that explain the history and importance of these iconic roadways.

Iowa is also known for its part in the U.S. political system. In the 1800s, Iowans and others held small meetings in their homes to discuss their feelings about their region and the country. Instead of holding **primaries** to nominate political candidates, Iowans decided to hold meetings called caucuses. They still hold caucuses to choose U.S. presidential candidates. The Iowa presidential caucus came to national prominence in 1972 when it was rescheduled as the first nominating contest of the presidential campaign.

The Land

Iowa ranks number one in the United States for corn and soybean production.

Iowa is **Native American** word meaning **"This Is the Place"** or **"The Beautiful Land."**

Iowa has more than **65 state parks** and **recreation areas**.

The Omaha and Oto Native American groups helped Lewis and Clark on their way through Iowa and the Midwest.

Beginnings

The name Iowa is from the Native American group with the same name who once lived in the area. Iowa was first explored by Europeans when French explorers moving up and down the Mississippi River and its tributaries made their way into the region. In 1673, Louis Jolliet and Father Jacques Marquette began exploring what is now known as Pikes Peak State Park.

Trappers and traders were the first European inhabitants of Iowa. The early trading posts would eventually turn into towns and then small cities. After the **Louisiana Purchase** in 1803, which added the area of Iowa and many other states to the United States, President Thomas Jefferson sent Meriwether Lewis and William Clark to explore the area. It was not until after 1833 that settlers began to populate the state in larger numbers. They came as family units from other states to establish homesteads and claim open farm land.

Where is IOWA?

Iowa shares its borders with Minnesota to the north, Wisconsin and Illinois to the east, Missouri to the south, and Nebraska and South Dakota to the west. Traveling through Iowa is simple thanks to the state's many roadways and airports. The state's rural road system connects its sparse population, which is spread over 55,869 square miles.

United States Map

Iowa

Alaska   Hawai'i

MAP LEGEND

- ⬛ Iowa
- ☆ Capital City
- ● Major City
- ▲ Effigy Mounds
- Iowa Great Lakes
- ▲ Amana Colonies
- ☐ Bordering States
- ☐ Water

NEBRASKA

MISSOURI

① Des Moines

Des Moines is the capital of Iowa. When Iowa became a state in 1846, Iowa City was the capital. Eleven years later, the capital was moved to Des Moines. Situated where the Des Moines and Raccoon Rivers meet, Des Moines is also more centrally located in the state.

② Amana Colonies

The seven Amana Colonies offer visitors the chance to experience locally crafted foods, furniture, and art inspired by the town's German roots. Located in east-central Iowa, the colonies cover 26,000 acres and were settled in 1855. Many of the residents are descendants of the original German colonists.

MINNESOTA

WISCONSIN

IOWA

4

2

△Amana Colonies

☆Des Moines

1

ILLINOIS

N

SCALE

0   50 miles

3 **Iowa Great Lakes**

The Iowa Great Lakes are located in Dickinson County and are a popular vacation destination. Spirit, West Okoboji, East Okoboji, and Silver Lakes all have glacial origins. The largest body of water is Lake Spirit, which is 4 miles long and 3 miles wide.

4 **Effigy Mounds**

Located in the Upper Mississippi River Valley, this national monument features about 20 ancient burial mounds built by early Native Americans. This site is considered sacred by many Native groups. Visitors can hike the area and enjoy the quiet beauty of the park.

Land Features

During the last Ice Age, huge **glaciers** covered the land that is now Iowa, as well as much of the Midwest. The heavy weight of the glaciers pressed down on the land, flattening it out. When the glaciers melted, the area was left with rich soil.

Today, Iowa has a prairie landscape of rolling hills and sloping valleys. It is part of the U.S. region called the Central Lowland, which consists of plains, hills, and excellent farmland. Despite Iowa's generally flat landscape, parts of the state contain ridges, cliffs, and steep valleys. Many streams and rivers crisscross Iowa, but the Mississippi and Missouri Rivers are by far the largest in the state. These rivers make up Iowa's eastern and western borders. Other important rivers in the state are the Big Sioux, Des Moines, and Cedar.

Flat Plains

A large expanse of flat land covers much of north-central Iowa. The region's soil is fertile and full of nutrients important for growing crops.

Prairie

Vast prairies of grasses and flowers once covered much of Iowa. Residents have restored and reconstructed much of the prairie that was lost.

Loess Hills

The rolling Loess Hills in western Iowa were formed over a long period of time from deposits of windblown soil.

Malanaphy Springs State Preserve

Located along the Upper Iowa River, Malanaphy Springs was dedicated as a state preserve in 1994 because of its geological features, including cascading falls and high cliffs.

Climate

Iowa's climate is extreme, with temperatures that sometimes drop below 0° Fahrenheit in the winter and soar above 100°F in the summer. January temperatures average 14°F in the northwest and 22°F in the southeast. Average summer temperatures range from 72°F in the north to 76°F in the south.

The hottest temperature recorded was 118°F at Keokuk on July 20, 1934. The coldest temperature was –47°F at Washta on January 12, 1912, and again at Elkader on February 3, 1996. There can be severe thunderstorms in the spring and summer, with hail, high winds, and heavy rain. The state averages 46 tornadoes each year.

Average Annual Precipitation Across Iowa

The average annual precipitation varies for different areas across Iowa. What problems might people have if their area got too much rain, and what could they do to solve these problems?

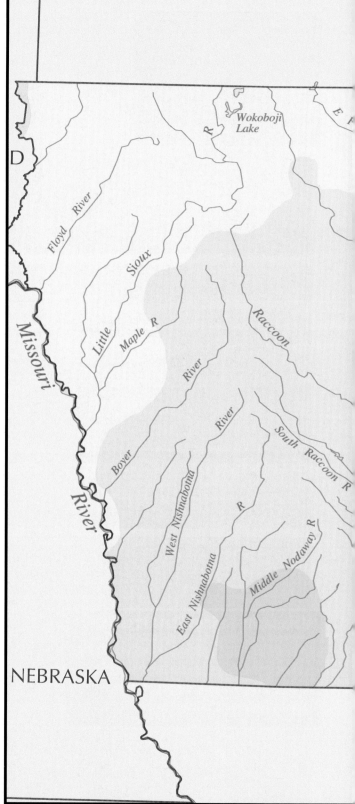

LEGEND

Average Annual Precipitation (in inches) 1961-1990

200 – 100.1

100 – 25.1

25 – 5 and less

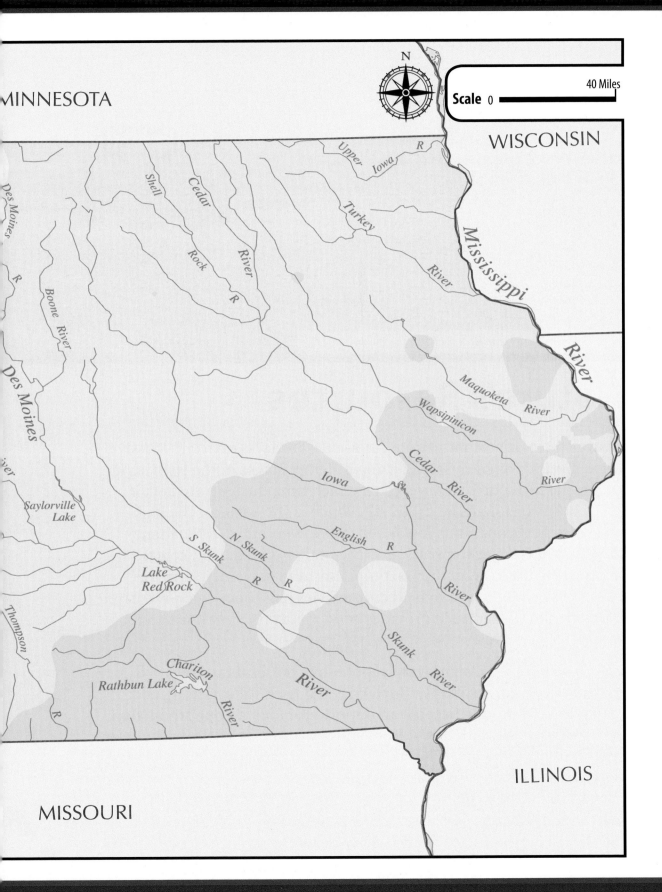

MINNESOTA

WISCONSIN

N

Des Moines R

Boone River

Shell

Cedar

Rock

River

R

Upper Iowa R

Turkey River

Mississippi

River

Des Moines

River

Saylorville Lake

Maquoketa River

Wapsipinicon

Cedar River

River

Iowa

English R

River

S Skunk R

N Skunk R

Lake Red Rock

Thompson

Chariton

Rathbun Lake

River

River

Skunk River

R

MISSOURI

ILLINOIS

Iowa harvested more than 8.5 million acres of soybeans in 2007.

Nature's Resources

Iowa's most important natural resource is its dark, rich soil. Massive ice sheets covered the area during different stages of the last Ice Age, which ended about 10,000 years ago. Each time the ice retreated, it left deposits of a material called silt, which is the basis for the high-quality soils. At one time, Iowa's soils were even more fertile than they are today. Over the years, overuse of the soil led to a decrease in productivity. In recent years, proper farm management and the development and use of **hybrid** crop species have once again increased productivity. Hybrid corn provides good **yields** because it is hardier and easier to harvest.

Iowa once produced significant supplies of coal, and there are still coal **reserves**. Early settlers mined coal and used it for heating and cooking. Coal mining became an important industry, but production declined after the mid-1900s. Iowa still gets most of its electricity from coal-fired power plants. The state has also taken steps to harness its **renewable** resources, such as wind and solar energy. In 2007, the state created an Office of Energy Independence, which is charged with managing the Iowa Power Fund. The goals of this fund are to increase the state's energy efficiency and use of clean energy technology.

Gypsum mines can be found in Webster, Iowa. This mineral is used to make construction material and fertilizer.

About 25 percent of the state's energy is produced by wind power.

Vegetation

Many of the grasses and flowers that once covered Iowa's prairies were cleared to make way for new farmland. Some prairie flowers can still be found in ditches and roadsides across the state. Iowa's beautiful wildflowers include the pasque flower, aster, phlox, lily, and wild indigo broom. The wild rose grows throughout the state. Tall, thick fields of prairie grasses such as sideoats grama once covered 80 percent of Iowa. Prairies are unique ecosystems. The plants, soil, and animal life all work together to create a specific environment not found in many locations.

Many of Iowa's original trees have been cut down, but more than 2.8 million acres of forestland remain. The eastern red cedar is the only evergreen tree that is native to every county in Iowa. Although it no longer thrives in the same numbers as it once did along the Cedar River, it can still be found across the prairie in the **windbreaks** for farms. Other native trees in Iowa include the white pine, balsam fir, and common juniper.

Wild Rose

The wild rose was chosen as Iowa's state flower in 1897. The flower, which grows throughout the state, blooms from June through late September.

Big Bluestem

Tall prairie grasses such as the big bluestem can grow to 12 feet high. This type of prairie grass once dominated the Iowa landscape.

Eastern Red Cedar

Despite its name, the eastern red cedar is not a cedar tree but a member of the juniper family. Its berries provide food for birds.

Pasque Flower

This prairie wildflower blooms in March and April. Native Americans used its crushed leaves for medicine.

Wildlife

Iowa's animals include white-tailed deer, muskrats, raccoons, coyotes, and foxes. Other small animals in the state include opossums, skunks, groundhogs, rabbits, badgers, minks, and weasels. The most common snakes are garter snakes, fox snakes, and bullsnakes, although timber rattlesnakes are found in some areas. Timber rattlesnakes are very large, often reaching lengths of 5 feet or more. Since they are venomous, they can be very dangerous.

Iowans can look to the skies for more wildlife. Crows, blue jays, cardinals, sparrows, doves, and kingfishers all live in Iowa. Bird watchers can also spot migrating birds flying south for the winter or north for the summer. Iowa lies along the path of the Mississippi Flyway, which is a north–south migratory route used by millions of birds. Mallards, Canada geese, blue-winged teal, and redheads are among the birds that fly through Iowa.

Opossum

The opossum is found throughout Iowa. Adults can grow to 34 inches long. The average litter size is seven, but litters can be much larger.

Coyote

The coyote is found throughout Iowa. The animal eats a variety of foods, including small mammals, birds, snakes, fruits, and vegetables.

Eastern Goldfinch

The Eastern goldfinch, Iowa's state bird, is also called the wild canary. The bird stays in Iowa even during cold winters.

White-tailed Deer

Deer are generally found in wooded areas. They also live in marshes and grassy places.

Economy

Madison County Covered Bridges

The popular book and movie *The Bridges of Madison County* turned the area into a popular destination. The six covered bridges within Madison are on the National Register of Historic Places.

Tourism

Iowa's natural beauty is on display to travelers throughout the state. Visitors can take a leisurely drive on the Loess Hills Scenic Byway in western Iowa. They can also paddle a canoe down the Inkpaduta Canoe Trail. This trail winds 134 miles down the Little Sioux River.

Those interested in history can visit the Effigy Mounds National Monument to see the burial mounds created by the people who lived in the region thousands of years ago. On the other side of Iowa, tourists can visit Old Fort Madison, situated on the Mississippi River. At the fort, historic interpreters recreate life on Iowa's rugged frontier.

Field of Dreams Movie Site

The 1999 movie *Field of Dreams* was filmed in Dyersville. The site attracts many baseball fans who visit the baseball diamond created for the film.

Lewis and Clark State Park

Located in Onawa, Lewis and Clark State Park features a full-size replica of the wooden boat that the explorers used to travel up the Missouri River.

Loess Hills Scenic Byway

The Loess Hills Scenic Byway is a series of roads running north to south in western Iowa. A variety of landscapes can be seen, including hills covered with prairie grass and wildflowers.

In 2014, Iowa farmers harvested nearly 2.4 million bushels of corn.

Primary Industries

Industry in Iowa is closely linked to the needs of the farming sector. The earliest industries were based on mills used to grind wheat into flour. When the price of wheat dropped at the end of the Civil War, farmers turned to growing corn and to raising hogs and cattle. As a result, corn-processing plants and pork-packing plants developed. Creameries sprang up to process cow's milk into butter.

Today, Iowa has a strong manufacturing industry. In fact, manufacturing accounts for a greater percentage of Iowa's income than farming. Much of the manufacturing in Iowa is still directly related to agriculture, in the form of food processing and the manufacturing of farm machinery. Other products manufactured in Iowa include refrigeration equipment, laundry equipment, plastics, electronic materials, motor homes, rolled aluminum, writing instruments, and small appliances.

Iowa is home to **more than 20 million hogs** and nearly **4 million head** of **cattle.**

As much as **one-fourth** of Iowa's exported **farm products** feed people overseas.

Value of Goods and Services (in Millions of Dollars)

Iowa has a strong manufacturing industry, although other areas contribute more money to the state's economy. Why would wholesale and retail trade be an important part of the state's economy?

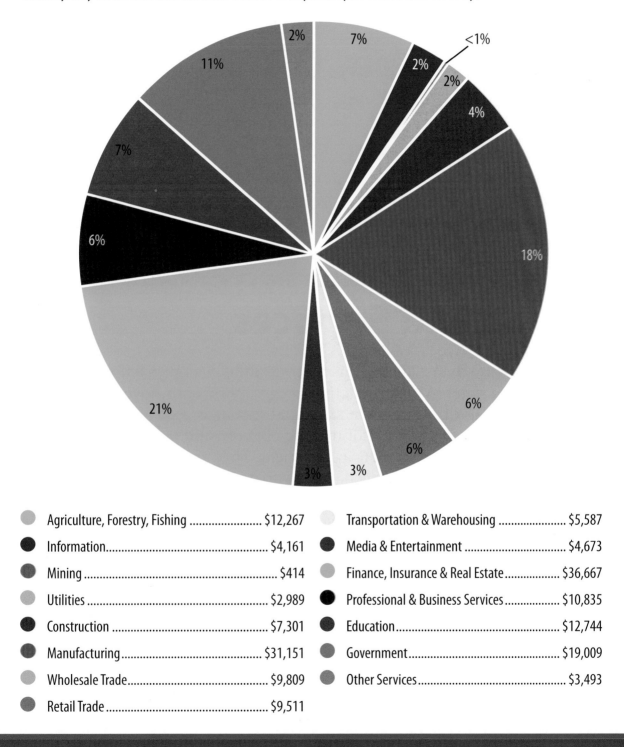

⬤ Agriculture, Forestry, Fishing	$12,267	⬤ Transportation & Warehousing	$5,587
⬤ Information	$4,161	⬤ Media & Entertainment	$4,673
⬤ Mining	$414	⬤ Finance, Insurance & Real Estate	$36,667
⬤ Utilities	$2,989	⬤ Professional & Business Services	$10,835
⬤ Construction	$7,301	⬤ Education	$12,744
⬤ Manufacturing	$31,151	⬤ Government	$19,009
⬤ Wholesale Trade	$9,809	⬤ Other Services	$3,493
⬤ Retail Trade	$9,511		

Nearly one-third of the state's grain harvest goes toward feeding pigs.

Goods and Services

There are more than 92,000 farms in Iowa, and Iowa ranks among the leading states in the production of eggs, pork, corn, soybeans, and beef. The majority of the corn raised in the state is used to feed livestock, but some of it is used for making popcorn and other foods. Soybeans also give Iowa's farmers a great yield. They are used to make food products, livestock feed, and a variety of goods, such as soap, cosmetics, and plastics. Iowa also has success producing several varieties of hay, including alfalfa, red clover, and Timothy.

Iowa is a national leader in the production of livestock and beef. In 2007, Iowa's dairy industry produced 4.3 billion pounds of milk, making Iowa one of the leading states for milk production. Most of the milk is made into butter and cream. Some farmers raise poultry and make their living from the sale of turkeys, chickens, and eggs. In 2007, there were 66.9 million chickens in Iowa. They laid about 13.9 billion eggs.

Government agencies, such as Iowa's Department of Economic Development, sponsor trade missions to encourage economic growth and to maintain the state's economy. Agriculture is assisted by research at Iowa's universities and colleges. Schools such as Iowa State University offer courses of study in agriculture and veterinary medicine. Despite the continuing importance of agriculture in Iowa, service industries now employ far more of the state's residents. Education, banking, health care, and insurance are important parts of the economy's service sector.

Students from all over the United States and more than 100 different countries attend Iowa State University.

The Seed Saver Exchange in Iowa works to protect and grow endangered garden and food crops by collecting and sharing seeds.

History

The Iowa grew corn, beans, and squash in their village gardens.

The Mound Builders built mounds shaped like animals, such as bears and birds. Some mounds in Iowa can still be seen today.

Native Americans

The first people to inhabit the area that now includes Iowa did so between 2,500 and 10,000 years ago, after the last glaciers disappeared. The Mound Builders constructed huge dirt mounds that they used for burial ceremonies and for defense. They also left behind evidence of stone carvings, pottery, weaving, and trade systems.

About 17 Native American groups lived in the area of Iowa at different times. One of the groups that once lived in the area gave its name to the state. The Iowa, or Ioway, people were both hunters and farmers, using farming techniques that they learned from neighboring Native American groups. They lived most of the year in permanent earthen houses. When they hunted, they lived in tepees. The Iowa spoke a language that was related to the Sioux language. They traded furs and clay pipes with the French.

After settlers began arriving in the region, the Iowa people surrendered to the United States following a series of conflicts in the 1800s. In 1836, they left their land in Iowa to the settlers and moved west. Today, the Iowa maintain a reservation along the Missouri River, on the border of Kansas and Nebraska.

Exploring the Land

Father Jacques Marquette and explorer Louis Jolliet are believed to be the first Europeans to arrive in what is now Iowa. Marquette was a Catholic missionary born in France. In 1672, he joined an expedition headed by Jolliet, a fur trader who had explored and charted much of the area around the Great Lakes. The goal of the expedition was to explore the areas now known as Minnesota, Iowa, and Illinois. Joined by five other explorers, Marquette and Jolliet crossed Lake Michigan and the Fox and Wisconsin Rivers. Then they followed the Mississippi River south to Iowa, where they arrived in June 1673.

Timeline of Settlement

U.S. Explorations and Settlements

1803 As part of the Louisiana Purchase, the United States, under President Thomas Jefferson, buys from France the huge Louisiana Territory west of the Mississippi River, including what is now Iowa.

1788 Julien Dubuque establishes a lead-mining operation with the Fox people near what is now Dubuque.

1682 La Salle explores the Mississippi River and claims the entire region for France.

1673 Father Jacques Marquette, accompanied by Louis Jolliet, arrives in Iowa and encounters Native Americans there.

1808 Fort Madison is founded by the U.S. Army.

European Exploration

In the early 1680s, French explorer René-Robert Cavelier, sieur de La Salle, surveyed the area. He was the first European to voyage down the Mississippi River to the Gulf of Mexico. As a result of this exploration, France laid claim to the entire Mississippi Valley under the name of the Louisiana Territory, which included the land that became Iowa. Years later, when the United States purchased the Louisiana Territory from France, Lewis and Clark explored the land during their famous expedition.

1834 Fort Des Moines is established.

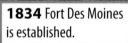

Territory and Statehood

1838 The Iowa Territory is established.

1832 The Native Americans lose the Black Hawk War, which allows settlers of European descent to inhabit northeast Iowa.

1838 Burlington becomes the first territorial capital.

1841 Iowa City becomes the territorial capital.

1846 Iowa enters the Union as the 29th state.

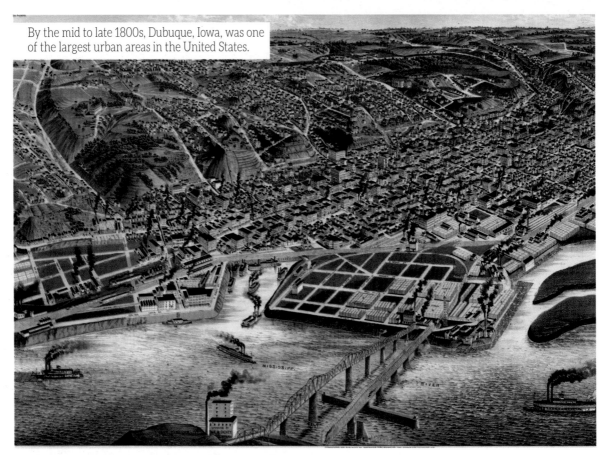

By the mid to late 1800s, Dubuque, Iowa, was one of the largest urban areas in the United States.

The First Settlers

Julien Dubuque was Iowa's first settler of European heritage. He was a French Canadian who arrived near what is now the city of Dubuque in 1788. After receiving permission from the Fox people, Dubuque started an operation mining lead. Dubuque hired the Fox to work in the mines. Dubuque and the Fox enjoyed good relations until his death in 1810.

Settlers sought to take over land belonging to the Native Americans. In 1832, Black Hawk, the chief of the Sauk, led his people and the Fox in what became known as the Black Hawk War. The U.S. Army won, and the Native Americans gave the United States a strip of land west of the Mississippi, called the Black Hawk Purchase. Settlement then began in earnest. Before 1832, there were fewer than 100 settlers of European descent in Iowa, but by 1840, that number had jumped to more than 43,000.

In 1835, when the U.S. Army sent soldiers to scout the Iowa area, the grass on the prairies was so high the soldiers could wrap it over their horses' backs and tie it in knots. The wild strawberries were so dense that they stained the horses' hooves red. Plowing the land for the first time was backbreaking work for the early settlers. The roots of the prairie grasses were extremely thick. When they were torn from the ground, it sounded like pistol shots. The early settlers farmed on 160-acre sections of land that were divided into quarters. The quarter sections formed an evenly divided grid of farms and small towns across the entire state. As a result of this land organization, most of the roads in the state run north–south or east–west.

The Julien Dubuque Monument sits on a bluff above the Catfish Creek. It was built as a memorial to the French and Native American fur trading culture and the first lead mines.

The Black Hawk War in 1832 began when a group of Sauk crossed the Mississippi River from Iowa into Illinois to resettle on disputed Native American land.

History Makers

Many notable Iowans contributed to the development of their state and country. They include a president, scientists, and leaders in the fight for equality. Advances in farming and satellite technology both have roots in Iowa.

Carrie Chapman Catt (1859–1947)

Carrie Chapman Catt, born as Carrie Lane, moved to Iowa from her native Wisconsin when she was 7. She graduated from Iowa State College and worked as a teacher, school superintendent, and reporter. In 1887, she joined the Iowa Woman **Suffrage** Association. Catt became a leader in the suffrage movement around the world and played a major role in the passage of the 19th Amendment to the U.S. Constitution in 1920, giving women the right to vote nationwide. That same year, she also established the League of Women Voters.

Herbert Hoover (1889–1974)

Herbert Hoover was born in West Branch. He was orphaned when he was 9 and then lived in Oklahoma and Oregon. A Republican, he was elected president in 1928. The **Great Depression** began the next year, and his policies were criticized for not doing enough to help the country. He lost his bid for reelection in 1932.

Henry A. Wallace (1888–1965)

Henry Wallace was born in Adair County and was raised on a farm. He graduated from Iowa State College and became an expert in plant **genetics**, developing types of high-yield hybrid corn and founding the world's leading seed corn company. From January 1941 to January 1945, he was Franklin Delano Roosevelt's vice president.

James Van Allen (1914–2006)

James Van Allen was born in Mount Pleasant. He taught physics at the University of Iowa for many years. Van Allen was an important figure in the launching of satellites by the United States. In 1958, he discovered radiation belts around Earth that are now called Van Allen belts.

Norman Borlaug (1914–2009)

Norman Borlaug was born on a farm near Cresco. He developed a high-yield type of wheat that was resistant to disease. He also became a central figure in producing new types of cereal and improving crop management practices to feed the hungry people in the world. He received the Nobel Peace Prize in 1970.

Culture

The annual Iowa State Fair features nearly 200 food stands and includes livestock shows, carnival rides, and musical performances.

More than 90 percent of high school students in Iowa graduate within four years.

The People Today

The twentieth century saw Iowa's population change from mainly rural to mainly urban. Many people moved to cities when farmers began replacing workers with machines. In the 1930s, about 60 percent of Iowa's people lived in rural areas. Now, about 40 percent of the people live in rural areas.

At the time of the census, Iowa was the 30th most-populous state in the country. It had a population density of 54 people per square mile, which was considerably lower than the national average of 87 people per square mile. Most Iowans were born in the state.

In terms of ancestry, people of European heritage make up the vast majority of the population. Less than 3 percent of the population is African American. Less than 2 percent is Asian American, and less than 1 percent is Native American. Hispanic Americans, who may be of any race, make up almost 5 percent of Iowa's population.

The population of Iowa **increased** in 2010 by more than **120,000 people**.

Q Why might people from other states and countries relocate to Iowa?

The capitol building is also home to Iowa's state law library.

State Government

Iowa's government is based on its state constitution. Like the U.S. Constitution, the state constitution divides the government into three parts. They are the executive, legislative, and judicial branches. The executive branch enforces the laws of the state and includes the governor and other executives.

The legislative branch is divided into the House of Representatives, which has 100 members, and the Senate, which has 50 members. Together, they form the General Assembly, which creates Iowa's laws. The judicial branch governs the court system. Seven judges rule on cases in the state's Supreme Court, which is the highest court in the state. There are also other lower-level courts in the state.

At the local level, Iowa has 99 counties. Each county is run by a board of supervisors, who are elected by county citizens. Iowa towns and cities also have their own governments, most run by mayors and city councils.

Iowa has elected mainly Republican candidates to office since the state's early days. From 1848, when Iowa first chose people to serve in the U.S. Senate, through 2010, Iowa has sent only 11 Democrats to the U.S. Senate, out of a total of 37 senators. However, Tom Harkin, a Democrat, was elected as one of Iowa's U.S. senators in 1984. He was reelected in 1990, 1996, 2002, and 2008.

The central dome of the Iowa State Capitol is made of iron and brick and covered with 23-karat gold.

Terry Branstad took office in 2011, becoming the state's 42nd governor.

Iowa's state song is called
"The Song of Iowa."

*You asked what land I love
the best, Iowa, 'tis Iowa,
The fairest State of all the
west, Iowa, O! Iowa,
From yonder Mississippi's stream
To where Missouri's waters gleam
O! fair it is as poet's dream,
Iowa, in Iowa.*

*See yonders fields of tasseled corn,
Iowa in Iowa,
Where plenty fills her golden horn,
Iowa in Iowa,
See how her wonderous praries shine.
To yonder sunset's purpling line,
O! happy land, O! land of mine,
Iowa, O! Iowa.*

* excerpted

The Tulip Festival in Pella, Iowa, celebrates the area's Dutch heritage every year.

Celebrating Culture

In the second half of the 1800s and the early part of the 1900s, many immigrants moved to Iowa. Immigrants of European descent included Germans, Scandinavians, Croatians, and Czechs, as well as people from Holland, Ireland, and Great Britain. In the early 1900s, African Americans from the South migrated to the northern and midwestern industrial states in search of work. Many settled in Iowa's larger cities, such as Des Moines and Waterloo. In recent years, new waves of immigrants have moved to the state to work in farming.

The settlement known as the Amana Colonies in the eastern part of Iowa was founded by a German religious community that migrated from Buffalo, New York, in 1855. Amana was one of the many experiments in **communal** living of the mid-1800s. In 1932, the people of the Amana Colonies voted to end their communal lifestyle. They reorganized themselves as a corporation called the Amana Society, which operated farms and factories. The Amana Church Society was created to maintain the group's religious beliefs.

Many Amish people live near Iowa City and Independence. The Amish hold beliefs that often conflict with modern technological practices. Their religious and social traditions include living simple lives without automobiles, electricity, telephones, or other modern conveniences. The Amish live in isolated communities and speak a unique type of German. The Amish are pacifists, which means that they do not believe in violence.

Lamoni, in southern Iowa, is the site of a **Mormon** community. The town was founded in the mid-1800s when Mormons passed through Iowa on their way to Utah to escape **persecution** in other states. Some Mormons settled in the area and established a community. Iowa is also home to members of a religious group called Quakers. The Quakers of the Springdale–West Branch area assisted with the Underground Railroad, a network of people who helped slaves escape from the South before the Civil War.

The seven villages of the Amana Colonies are now a popular tourist destination. The Colonies offer attractions based on handcrafted goods and locally-sourced food.

The largest Amish and Mennonite settlement in Iowa is located just outside of Kalona. The Amish life is centered around rural living, especially farming.

Iowa native John Wayne appeared in nearly 250 movies.

Arts and Entertainment

Grant Wood is perhaps Iowa's best-known artist. Born in 1892 near Anamosa, Wood was one of the leaders of the regionalist art movement. Regionalist artists were known for their paintings of everyday rural life. Wood's painting *American Gothic* is considered one of the most recognizable paintings from the United States. Wood remained loyal to Iowa throughout his life and even taught art in the public schools of Cedar Rapids.

Iowa's colleges and universities are cultural centers that attract symphonies, dance companies, and musical shows from around the world. Iowa showed its commitment to the arts by establishing the first creative-writing degree in the United States. The Iowa Writers' Workshop got its start at the University of Iowa in 1936. Since then, the program has served as a model for other programs at universities across North America.

Ashton Kutcher was born in **Cedar Rapids, Iowa,** and named one of *Time* magazine's Top 100 **Most Influential People** in 2010.

John Wayne was born in **Winterset, Iowa** and appeared in nearly **250 movies.**

Some well-known performers have come from Iowa. John Wayne, a popular and rugged movie star, was best known for his roles in Hollywood Western films, such as *Stagecoach*, *Fort Apache*, and *The Searchers*. He was born in Winterset in 1907. Other performers born in Iowa include television talk show host Johnny Carson and showman William Cody, who was known as Buffalo Bill. More recent performers born in Iowa include actor and producer Ashton Kutcher, who starred in *That '70s Show* and *Punk'd*. Elijah Wood, who starred in *The Lord of the Rings* movies, is from Cedar Rapids.

Native Iowan Grant Wood was known for painting local subjects in a realistic manner. His painting *American Gothic* is currently on display at the Art Institute of Chicago.

Iowa has also produced a number of talented writers. Hamlin Garland, Wallace Stegner, Susan Glaspell, Elsa Maxwell, David Rabe, and MacKinlay Kantor all came from the state. Advice columnists Ann Landers and Abigail van Buren were twin sisters from Sioux City. Meredith Willson, who wrote the popular musical *The Music Man*, was born in Mason City. The show is set in the fictional Iowa town of River City, which is based on his hometown.

The Music Man has won five Tony Awards, including Best Musical.

The Hawkeyes are the University of Iowa's football team. They play their home games at Kinnick Stadium in Iowa City.

Sports and Recreation

Sporting events are extremely popular in Iowa. Although the state has no professional teams at the major-league level, there are many lower-level teams. In addition, college sports are very popular. The University of Iowa's sports teams, called the Hawkeyes, draw large crowds. Hawkeye football and basketball games are especially popular. The Hawkeyes are not just athletes. They also excel in academics. Students who participate in athletics at the University of Iowa have been notable for also achieving academic success.

Many other Iowa colleges and universities have their own popular athletic programs. The Drake University Bulldogs regularly do well in a variety of sports, including football, basketball, soccer, softball, volleyball, and track. Drake University hosts the annual Drake Relays, one of the premier track and field meets in the Midwest.

Two-time NFL Most Valuable Player, **Kurt Warner**, was born in Burlington, Iowa, in 1971.

The Hawkeye wrestling team at the **University of Iowa** has **won** the **national college championship** more than **20 times**.

Every year, the Des Moines Register sponsors RAGBRAI, which stands for the Register's Annual Great Bicycle Ride Across Iowa. This seven-day event, which began in 1973, is now the world's oldest, longest, and largest bicycle touring event. The ride begins in a town in western Iowa and ends in a town in eastern Iowa, with stops along the way. Since the event is so popular, those wishing to participate must apply.

More than 8,500 people participate in RAGBRAI every year.

The Loess Hills afford many Iowans the opportunity for hiking, backpacking, and camping.

Get To Know
IOWA

THE FIRST BREAD SLICING MACHINE TO CUT AN ENTIRE LOAF AT ONCE WAS INVENTED IN DAVENPORT, IOWA.

Visitors to **Strawberry Point**, Iowa, can visit a 15-foot strawberry sculpture, the world's **largest strawberry**.

Snake Alley, located in Burlington, Iowa, is the *MOST CROOKED STREET* in the world.

Iowa has **more readers** than any other state in the United States.

In Iowa, hogs outnumber humans **four** to **one**.

THE RINGLING BROTHERS, WHO CREATED ONE OF THE LARGEST CIRCUSES IN THE U.S., WERE BORN IN MCGREGOR, IOWA.

The **largest Amish** community west of the **Mississippi River** is located in **Kalona, Iowa.**

Brain Teasers

What have you learned about Iowa after reading this book? Test your knowledge by answering these questions. All of the information can be found in the text you just read. The answers are provided below for easy reference.

1 In what year did Iowa become a state?

2 Who are believed to be the first Europeans to arrive in what is now Iowa?

3 What was the first territorial capital of Iowa?

4 Which prairie grass in Iowa can grow up to 12 feet high?

5 In which Iowa town was Herbert Hoover born?

6 Who is Iowa's best-known artist?

7 What is the highest temperature ever recorded in Iowa?

8 Which chief of the Sauk led his people and the Fox against the U.S. Army in 1832?

Key Words

communal: a type of lifestyle in which all items and possessions are shared within a community

genetics: the study of how characteristics are passed down from generation to generation

glaciers: large masses of slow-moving ice

Great Depression: a huge decline in the world economy that lasted from 1929 until 1939, with widespread unemployment and poverty

hybrid: a plant or animal that is a combination of two different plants or animals

Louisiana Purchase: a large area purchased from France by the United States in 1803

Mormon: a follower of a religion founded by Joseph Smith in 1830

persecution: being attacked for one's beliefs

primaries: elections to choose candidates to run in the general election

renewable: a resource that can be used over and over without being depleted

reserves: supplies

suffrage: the right to vote

windbreaks: trees or bushes that are planted to provide shelter from the wind

yields: the amount of a crop produced by cultivation per unit of land area

Index

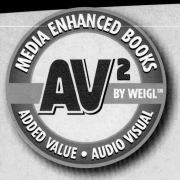

Log on to www.av2books.com

AV² by Weigl brings you media enhanced books that support active learning. Go to www.av2books.com, and enter the special code found on page 2 of this book. You will gain access to enriched and enhanced content that supplements and complements this book. Content includes video, audio, weblinks, quizzes, a slide show, and activities.

AV² Online Navigation

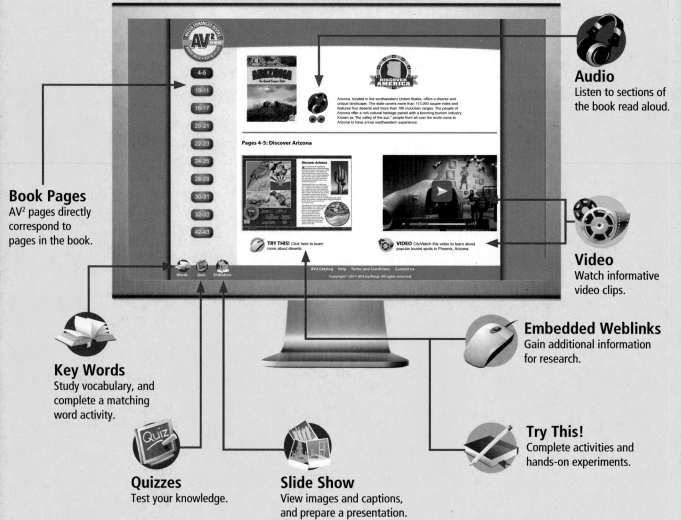

Book Pages
AV² pages directly correspond to pages in the book.

Audio
Listen to sections of the book read aloud.

Video
Watch informative video clips.

Key Words
Study vocabulary, and complete a matching word activity.

Embedded Weblinks
Gain additional information for research.

Quizzes
Test your knowledge.

Slide Show
View images and captions, and prepare a presentation.

Try This!
Complete activities and hands-on experiments.

AV² was built to bridge the gap between print and digital. We encourage you to tell us what you like and what you want to see in the future.

Sign up to be an AV² Ambassador at www.av2books.com/ambassador.

Due to the dynamic nature of the Internet, some of the URLs and activities provided as part of AV² by Weigl may have changed or ceased to exist. AV² by Weigl accepts no responsibility for any such changes. All media enhanced books are regularly monitored to update addresses and sites in a timely manner. Contact AV² by Weigl at 1-866-649-3445 or av2books@weigl.com with any questions, comments, or feedback.